KT-171-146

MAMMALS

David Burnie

EAST SUSSEX COUNTY COUNCIL
WITHDRAWN
20 A

04247531

KINGFISHER

First published 2011 by Kingfisher
This paperback edition first published 2014 by Kingfisher
an imprint of Macmillan Children's Books
a division of Macmillan Publishers Limited
20 New Wharf Road, London N1 9RR
Basingstoke and Oxford
Associated companies throughout the world
www.panmacmillan.com

Illustrations by: Peter Bull Art Studio, Barry Croucher,
Gary Hanna (www.the-art-agency.co.uk)

ISBN 978-0-7534-3673-8

Copyright © Macmillan Children's Books 2011

All rights reserved. No part of this publication may be reproduced, stored
in or introduced into a retrieval system, or transmitted, in any form or by any means
(electronic, mechanical, photocopying, recording or otherwise), without the prior written
permission of the publisher. Any person who does any unauthorized act in relation to this
publication may be liable to criminal prosecution and civil claims for damages.

1 3 5 7 9 8 6 4 2
1TR/1113/WKT/UG/128MA

A CIP catalogue record for this book is available from the British Library.

Printed in China

This book is sold subject to the condition that it shall not, by way
of trade or otherwise, be lent, resold, hired out, or otherwise circulated
without the publisher's prior consent in any form of binding or cover
other than that in which it is published and without a similar condition
including this condition being imposed on the subsequent purchaser.

Note to readers: The website addresses listed in this book are correct at the time of publishing.
However, due to the ever-changing nature of the internet, website addresses and content can change.
Websites can contain links that are unsuitable for children. The publisher cannot be held responsible for
changes in website addresses or content, or for information obtained through third-party websites.
We strongly advise that internet searches should be supervised by an adult.

The Publisher would like to thank the following for permission to reproduce their material. Every care has been taken to trace copyright holders. However, if there have been unintentional omissions or failure to trace copyright holders, we apologise and will, if informed, endeavour to make corrections in any future edition. (t = top, b = bottom, c = centre, r = right, l = left):

Front cover t Shutterstock/EML; tr Shutterstock/Four Oaks; tc Shutterstock/Mihai Dancaescu; br Shutterstock/manfredxy; bl Olga Khoroshunova; c Shutterstock/Clickit; back cover r Shutterstock/Eric Isselee; l Alamy/ Eureka; and pages 4tr Photolibrary/Kelvin Aitken; 4cl Shutterstock/Mogens Trolle; 4c Shutterstock/Joy Brown; 4cr Frank Lane Picture Agency (FLPA)/Hugh Lansdown; 4br Shutterstock/Eric Isselee; 4–5t Naturepl/Brendon Cole; 4–5b Shutterstock/Susan Flashman; 5tr Roger Ingle/Flora & Fauna International; 5c Shutterstock/Sharon Morris; 5r Shutterstock/Milena; 5bl Ardea/John Daniels; 5br Naturepl/Anup Shah; 7tr FLPA/Michael & Patricia Fogden/Minden; 7bc Ardea/Jean Paul Ferrero; 8 Naturepl/Pete Oxford; 9 Photolibrary/All Canada Photos; 11tl Shutterstock/mlorenz; 11tr Photolibrary/Ronald Wittek; 12tl Naturepl/Dan Burton; 12tr Science Photo Library (SPL)/Paul Gunning; 12c Shutterstock/MikeE; 13tl Naturepl/John Downer; 13bl Alamy/blickwinkel; 13tr Photoshot/Nigel J Dennis/NHPA; 13cr Photoshot/Nigel J Dennis/NHPA; 14tr FLPA/Jurgen & Christine Sohns; 14cl Shutterstock/Patsy Michaud; 14b Shutterstock/H. Damke; 16tr Shutterstock/Larsek; 16cl Alamy/Paul Maguire; 16–17 Shutterstock/Gail Johnson; 17tl FLPA/ Michio Hoshino/Minden; 17tr FLPA/Imagebroker; 17br Alamy/Accent Alaska.com; 18tr SPL/Andrew Syred; 18c Photolibrary/OSF; 18bl Alamy/WorldFoto; 18–19 Shutterstock/Pichugin Dmitry; 19cl SPL/Andrew Syred; 19cr Photolibrary/John Pitcher; 19br Photolibrary/Animal Animal; 20tl Photolibrary/David Paynter; 20cl Alamy/Yvette Cardozo; 20c Shutterstock/palko72; 20b Shutterstock/EcoPrint; 20br DK Images; 21tl Photolibrary/ OSF; 21cl Corbis/Barbara Wilton; 21brl Shutterstock/Olga Selyutina; 21brc Shutterstock/Jeff Banke; 21brr Shutterstock/Jakub Krechowicz; 22tl Shutterstock/worldswildlifewonders; 22c FLPA/Nobert Wu/Minden; 23t FLPA/Flip Nicklin/Minden; 23tl DK Images; 23cl Naturepl/Doug Perrine; 23c Shutterstock/A J Gallant; 23bl Alamy/blickwinkel; 23tr FLPA/Lynn M Stone; 23cr Seapics/Richard Herrmann; 23b FLPA/Flip Nicklin/Minden; 25tr Naturepl/Mark Carwardine; 25b Getty Images; 26bl Shutterstock/lbsky; 27bl SPL/SPX; 27br Alamy/David Fleetham; 28t Alamy/Eclectic Images; 28 Alamy/Gallo Images and Shutterstock/neelsky and Shutterstock/ David Young; 28–29 Shutterstock/EcoPrint; 29tl FLPA/Imagebroker; 29tr FLPA/Gerard Lacz; 29cl Shutterstock/Graeme Shannon; 29c FLPA/Vincent Grafhorst/Minden; 29br FLPA/Ariadne Van Zandbergen; 30tl Alamy/ John Warburton-Lee; 30lct Shutterstock/worldswildlifewonders; 30lcb Alamy/Imagebroker; 30b Shutterstock/Eric Isselee; 30tr Alamy/Wolfgang Kaehler; 31tl Shutterstock/livestockimages; 31tr Photolibrary/Corbis; 31b Shutterstock/Sharon Morris; 32tc Shutterstock/javarman; 32cr Shutterstock/Norma Cornes; 32bl Shutterstock/Timothy Craig Lubcke; 33c Shutterstock/Kersti Joergensen; 33tr FLPA/Konrad Wothe/Mindenl 33bl FLPA/ Thomas Marent/Minden; 33br Alamy/Jonathan Hewitt; 34tr FLPA/Dembinsky Photo Association; 35bl FLPA/Michael & Patricia Fogden/Minden; 35br Photolibrary/Animal Animal; 36–37 FLPA/Thomas Mangelson/ Minden; 36br Photolibrary/Peter Arnold Images; 36br Shutterstock/Olga Khoroshunova; 37cl Naturepl/Steven Kazlowski; 37bl Photolibrary/fStop; 39bl Naturepl/Stephen Dalton; 39br FLPA/Konrad Wothe/Minden; 41bl Shutterstock/Four Oaks; 41br Photolibrary/Peter Arnold Images; 42tl Press Association/AP; 42tr Alamy/Images of Africa; 42b Alamy/Images of Africa; 43tcr Alamy/Frisk; 43tl Getty/Andrea Pistolesi; 43cl Alamy/ Images of Africa; 43cr Corbis/Olah Tibor/epa; 43br Andreas Whiting/A Mohamed/Cat News; 48tr Shutterstock/Sharon Morris; 48cl Alamy/John Elk III; 48cr Photolibrary/bios; 48bl Shutterstock/Christopher P Grant.

CONTENTS

WORLD OF MAMMALS

The first mammals lived side by side with the dinosaurs, more than 200 million years ago. Dinosaurs died out, but mammals survived to become the most successful animals on Earth. They vary hugely in size and live on land, in water and even in the air. But all mammals share three special features – they are warm-blooded, they have hair or fur, and they raise their young on milk.

Keeping warm

Most mammals are covered with fur, which helps to keep their bodies warm. Swimming mammals often have fat instead, just under their skin. A walrus's fat can be 15cm thick. It uses its bushy 'moustache' to find food on the seabed.

Unlike small bats, fruit bats are vegetarians, tracking down fruit by its colour and smell.

WARM-BLOODED – having a body temperature that stays warm and steady, whatever the conditions outside

Together with okapis, giraffes make up a small family of African mammals. They have long necks and tongues.

The elephant family includes three species – two from Africa and one from Asia.

Anteaters have long snouts without any teeth. They live on the ground or in trees.

> The world's lightest mammal is the Etruscan shrew. It weighs only about 2 grams.

We are family

Scientists divide mammals into about 150 different families. The mammals in some families, called marsupials, raise their young in a pouch. Others, called placentals, raise their young inside the mother's body. Placental mammals include humans, and also blue whales – the biggest animals that have ever lived.

⊖ NEW DISCOVERIES

So far, scientists have identified about 5,500 kinds of mammals, but new animals are still being discovered every year. They include the Annamite striped rabbit, with distinctively patterned fur, from the forests of Southeast Asia. It was first seen by scientists in 1999. It feeds at night, but little else is known about how it lives.

Annamite striped rabbit caught on camera

www.bbc.co.uk/nature/life/mammal

Orcas, or killer whales, have pointed teeth and hunt large prey.

Zebras belong to a large family of plant-eating mammals with a hard hoof on each foot.

Most lemurs live in trees, but the ring-tailed lemur spends a lot of its life on the ground.

The grey kangaroo is one of the largest marsupials. It can bound at speeds of up to 50km/h.

Brown rats are rodents – mammals with gnawing teeth.

Tigers belong to the cat family. Like most cats, they hunt on their own, and feed entirely on meat.

UTERUS – a muscle-lined bag that surrounds and protects a baby mammal inside its mother's body

muscles of uterus

The foal is surrounded by a bag containing amniotic fluid. This cushions the foal when its mother is on the move.

The developing foal receives food from the placenta – a spongy pad connected to the side of the uterus.

The fully formed foal in its mother's uterus, shortly before being born.

Into the outside world

A zebra foal develops inside its mother's uterus, or womb, over one year. During this time, it turns from a single cell into a complete, new animal, nourished by substances circulating in its mother's blood. Finally, the big day comes. Powerful muscles push the foal out of the mother's body. As the foal takes its first breaths, its mother licks the young zebra dry. Within minutes, the foal totters to its feet and starts to feed on its mother's milk.

Unlike a human baby, the newly born foal emerges feet-first.

STARTING LIFE

Few moments are as dramatic as a zebra's birth, when a young foal emerges onto Africa's grassy plains. Like most mammals, zebras develop inside their mothers, so they are already partly grown at birth. Other mammals start life in a different way. Marsupials are born hairless and blind, and develop in a pouch, while platypuses and echidnas hatch from tiny eggs. Despite these differences, all mammals start life on the same nutritious food: their mother's milk.

Egg-laying mammals
Platypuses and echidnas are the only mammals that lay eggs. This young echidna – or puggle – has hatched inside its mother's pouch and will stay safely inside it for at least six weeks.

Free ride

Some young mammals cling to their mother, using their claws to hold on to her fur. Female sloths hang upside down, so their babies can lie on them like a hammock.

Sloths usually have a single young, so there is plenty of room for it to travel aboard its mother.

Zebras usually lie down to give birth, but many other mammals give birth standing up.

⊖ EARLY BIRTH

Newborn kangaroos look like small, pink grubs. At first, only their front legs work. They use them to pull their way through their mother's fur and into her pouch. Here, the baby kangaroo, or joey, locks onto one of the female's teats, and starts to feed. Up to six months later, the joey finally moves out. Often, the next joey is already inside.

newly born joey

grey kangaroo with four-month-old joey

The newly born foal takes its first drink of milk.

A foal is born with an instinct to suck milk from its mother's teats, or nipples.

www.enchantedlearning.com/coloring/marsupial.shtml

A BETTER BITE

"If you can't bite, don't show your teeth."

Old Yiddish proverb

Reacting to danger, the puma reveals its fearsome teeth. Its backward-pointing ears are another warning sign, telling other animals not to come close.

Many animals have teeth, but only mammals have teeth that are differently shaped. Together, a mammal's teeth work like a toolkit, letting it deal with its food. Plant-eating mammals have teeth for biting and for chewing, while predatory kinds have teeth that can grip, slice, crush or even crack open bones. Predators sometimes use their teeth to drag away food – a grizzly bear's teeth are strong enough to move a horse.

Toothless mammals

Adult anteaters do not have any teeth. They do not need them, because they collect insects using their amazingly long tongue and then swallow them whole. Their stomach grinds up their food, helped by the grit that they eat.

🔘 TOOLS OF THE TRADE

Scientists often identify mammals from their skulls and teeth. A hyena's teeth crack open bones, while a dolphin's teeth are shaped for catching fish. The crab-eating seal has strangely round-lobed teeth. Despite its name, the seal feeds on tiny animals, using its teeth like a sieve.

Crab-eater seals have teeth with rounded lobes like stubby fingers.

Dolphins have dozens of long, pointed teeth.

Hyena teeth can shatter bones, which the hyena swallows and digests.

> Dolphins are the toothiest mammals. They have a single set of up to 252 teeth.

Muscles closing the jaws reach as far as the top of the head.

Grip and slice

The puma, or cougar, belongs to a group of mammals called carnivores, which feed on meat. They have long canines, or eye teeth, which are just the right shape for stabbing and gripping their prey. Behind them, blade-like teeth called carnassials slice through freshly killed flesh. Like most mammals, pumas have two sets of teeth. Their milk teeth have short roots and are replaced by bigger, permanent teeth as the pumas grow into adults.

The carnassials (red) are near the back of the mouth, where the bite is stronger. Canine teeth (yellow) are on either side of the incisors at the front of the mouth.

www.amnh.org/ology/features/stufftodo_zoology/superteeth.php

WEANING – the change from mother's milk to a more grown-up diet

Sharp vision picks up the slightest sign of movement against the snow.

Ears swivel back and forth to pick up sounds – a feature shared by dogs, which are descended from wolves.

HUNTING IN A PACK

Instead of hunting alone, grey wolves often live and hunt in packs. It is an efficient way of life, because it lets wolves prey on animals that are too big and too strong for them to tackle on their own. A pack usually contains up to 12 adult wolves, led by a dominant – or 'alpha' – pair. The dominant pair mate for life and produce all the pack's young. When they are too old to breed, younger members of the pack take their place.

Closing in

After a long chase through Canada's wintry landscape, a pack of wolves closes in on a moose. Moose are the world's largest deer – a big adult male can weigh more than 500kg, which is over ten times as much as an average Arctic wolf. But numbers and stamina count. Guided by their keen senses, the wolves move in to make the kill.

> Despite their bad reputation, wolves have hardly ever been known to attack people.

Call of the wild

Wolf packs stake out a territory so that they have enough space to hunt. They claim territory by marking it with scent, and by howling. Their eerie chorus keeps neighbouring packs away.

Something for everyone

After most hunts, all the wolves usually eat some part of the kill. Meat is carried back to the den for cubs that are being weaned. In good times, wolves bury half-eaten food, consuming it weeks or even months later.

Despite its powerful body, the moose is not a good fighter. Its antlers are for show, rather than for attack.

⊖ SNAP ATTACK

wolves surround the moose

moose's hindquarters vulnerable to attack

moose forced to stand its ground

The end of the hunt comes when the wolves surround the moose, cutting off its escape route. With the moose in snapping range, they dart forwards to bite its unprotected underside, or grip its muzzle tightly in their jaws. The moose spins around to fend off the attacks, but finally falls as the pack moves in.

www.arkive.org/grey-wolf/canis-lupus/

SELF-DEFENCE

At the first sign of trouble, most mammals try to make an emergency escape. Some run, while others swim or fly, but a small number (mostly plant-eaters) use special defences to hold their ground. They include pangolins, which have built-in armour plating, and also porcupines, which are protected by hundreds of hollow quills, which are long, stiff and very sharp. When fully raised, they can keep an adult lion at bay.

QUILLS - *in mammals, extra-large hairs with sharp points that are used in self-defence*

An African porcupine's quills have backward-facing barbs that catch on skin and make them hard to pull out.

> An African porcupine's quills can be 30cm long. American porcupines have shorter and softer quills.

Two against one

With its back facing danger, an African porcupine tries to fend off two hungry lions. The lions are intent on flipping it over, so they can reach its furry underside. Each time they move closer, the porcupine rattles its quills and reverses. The quills can detach easily, embedding themselves in a lion's skin.

Chemical defences
Performing a handstand, this skunk can squirt an evil-smelling fluid from glands beneath its tail. The fluid contains a high concentration of sulphur – the same substance that gives burning rubber its stomach-churning reek.

If quills get stuck in the skin, they remain embedded and can cause fatal wounds.

Like most cats, lions can extend and retract their claws. This makes sure they are always sharp.

⊖ ARMOUR PLATING

Millions of years ago, giant, armoured mammals roamed the Earth. Some were as big as cars. These giants eventually died out, but armoured mammals still exist today – including armadillos, which are covered in bony plates, and pangolins, which have overlapping scales. Some kinds roll up to protect soft body parts inside.

pangolin stops and tucks in its head when threatened

legs disappear beneath the pangolin's sharp-edged scales

tail curls up, hiding the legs and head, and completing the ball

www.awf.org/wildlife-conservation/porcupine

STRENGTH IN NUMBERS

RODENT – a mammal with four chisel-shaped incisors that grow non-stop

In many parts of the world, rodents outnumber all other mammals put together. There are more than 2,000 kinds, living almost everywhere on land, as well as in rivers, streams and ponds. Some are large, but most are small, fast-moving animals that try to keep out of sight. Rodents have sharp front teeth, and they gnaw through plants and seeds. Small rodents – such as mice and voles – breed at an amazing rate, but predators usually keep their numbers under control.

Productive parents

A female house mouse can have up to 80 babies a year. Blind and helpless at birth, her young grow up fast. By the age of ten weeks, they are fully mature and ready to have their own families.

golden-mantled ground squirrel

Cheeky

Like many small rodents, this North American ground squirrel has flexible cheek pouches, which work like shopping bags. It fills its pouches with seeds, and then scampers to its burrow to store them underground.

Beavers gnaw through trees up to 25cm across, using their incisor teeth. These flat-bladed teeth have a self-sharpening front edge and long roots that curve towards the back of the jaws.

North American beaver dam

Beaver fur is waterproofed by a strongly scented natural oil, produced in glands near the tail.

⊖ GIANT RODENTS

Capybaras are the world's largest rodents. Looking like giant guinea pigs, they live in marshy places in South America, where they feed on waterside plants. Adult males measure up to 1.3m long, and can weigh as much as an adult man. Capybaras are related to guinea pigs, so the resemblance is not just skin-deep. But a capybara is specially adapted for swimming, with slightly webbed feet, and eyes and nostrils high up on its head.

Capybaras have barrel-shaped bodies and short legs.

> The largest-known beaver dam, in Canada, is 850m long. It was found using satellite pictures in 2010.

"In time, a mouse will gnaw
through a cable."

Dutch and German proverb

Master builders

Many animals build their own homes, but beavers are
the only mammals that make dams across streams and
rivers. It is an immense task, and they do it to protect
their homes, or lodges, and to store winter food. To make
a dam, beavers cut down waterside trees and skilfully
float them into place. The dam is then sealed with mud
and clay. Large dams are made by several generations
of beavers, and can be more than 50 years old.

*The lodge is a hollow
mound of branches,
with concealed entrances
below the waterline.*

*Small eyes, positioned high
on the head, are covered
by see-through
membranes
when diving.*

*Beavers chew
through hard, old
wood – as well as
the soft saplings that
they eat – using
their powerful
jaw muscles.*

http://video.nationalgeographic.com/video/player/animals/beaver_lifecycle.html

FOLLOW THE LEADER

Hoofed mammals often spend their lives in herds. By staying together, they have a better chance of spotting danger, and less chance of being singled out and attacked. Wildebeest and caribou form herds hundreds of thousands strong, but in the past, some antelope herds contained ten million animals, and were more than 100km long. Today, many farm animals live in herds, which makes them easy to control.

Wildebeest have curved, hollow horns. During the breeding season, males sometimes use them to ram their rivals.

Each front hoof has a gland that leaves a trail of scent. Wildebeest can use the scent to find their way back to the herd.

Life on the move

Surrounded by clouds of dust, common wildebeest migrate across Africa's Serengeti plain. Every year, they travel up to 2,500km, letting them make the most of the seasonal rains. Wildebeest spend the dry season in wooded grassland, until instinct tells them that it is time to move. Gathering in immense lines, they stream across the landscape, giving birth to their calves on the way. By the time the wet season comes, the wildebeest arrive in lush grassland where they feast on the annual burst of food.

> Most wildebeest give birth in a three-week 'slot', so their young are almost exactly the same age as each other.

http://video.nationalgeographic.com/video/player/animals/wildebeest_migration.html

Swimming herds

In the Canadian Arctic, caribou spend winter in forests, and summer in the open tundra. Their journey can be up to 5,000km long – a record for a land mammal. On the way, they often have to swim across sea inlets and lakes.

Time out

Wildebeest give birth in the open and their young soon follow the herd. Most deer and gazelles are different. This baby deer, or fawn, was born in thick undergrowth. It will stay hidden until it is several weeks old.

Wildebeest travel together, or in mixed herds with other mammals such as gazelles and zebras.

Defensive circle

Musk oxen live in the far north, where the biggest danger comes from wolves. If a herd is threatened, the adults form a defensive circle, with their massive horns facing outwards and their young in the centre.

INSULATION – a body layer that helps to stop an animal becoming too warm or too cold

SURVIVING EXTREMES

Mammals live in some of the hottest, coldest, highest and driest places on Earth. Unlike humans, they do not have special equipment or clothing, but they do have physical features that help them to survive. These include amazingly warm fur, thick layers of body fat, and unusual body chemistry that lets them get all their water from their food.

Cells in the hump store fat – a substance that provides energy when food is hard to find.

Beating the heat

Like many small desert mammals, the long-eared jerboa digs burrows and avoids the daytime heat by feeding after dark. It eats seeds and insects, and survives on 'metabolic water' – water that it makes chemically from its food.

range: deserts of Central Asia, from Mongolia to China

High life

Vicuñas live at altitudes of up to 5,500m, where the oxygen in the air is extremely thin. Here, human hikers soon get tired, but vicuñas can run up steep slopes with ease. Their secret: special red blood cells that get the most oxygen from every breath.

range: Andes mountains, from Peru to Chile

> In the Arctic of northern Canada, some ground squirrels hibernate for nine months each year.

www.bbc.co.uk/nature/life/arctic_fox

Double protection

Bactrian camels live deep in Central Asia, where it is hot in summer and freezing in winter, and dry nearly all the time. They store fat in their two humps, and they keep warm because of a long winter coat, which falls off in large patches during spring.

range: deserts of
Central Asia, from
Mongolia to China

A camel's undercoat is made of fine hairs that trap air, creating an insulating layer that keeps its body warm.

Winter wrap

The Arctic fox is one of the world's most cold-proof mammals, thanks to its exceptionally thick winter fur. It can survive in temperatures as low as -50°C, using its bushy tail to protect its feet and face from the icy wind. In spring, its white winter coat is replaced by a much thinner one, coloured brownish-grey.

range: High Arctic,
in North America,
Europe and Asia

⊖ HIBERNATION

Instead of battling through the winter, some mammals hibernate instead. They look as though they are sleeping, but their bodies turn cold, and their hearts beat only a few times a minute. Like machines on standby, they need only a small amount of energy to stay alive. Rodents often hibernate in burrows, while bats often choose caves or abandoned mines.

little brown bats hibernating

IVORY – a hard substance found in mammal tusks

MODERN MAMMOTHS

Elephants are unique. No other mammals look like them or share their way of life. Weighing up to seven tonnes, they are the biggest land animals and the last survivors in a family that once included ice-age mammoths. Today, there are three species of these huge animals. In some places they are thriving, but in others they are threatened by illegal ivory hunters, as well as by a loss of forests and the spread of farms.

Party trick

Standing on its hind legs, a male African elephant reaches high into a tree. Its trunk is a multi-purpose tool. It can collect leaves, but the trunk can also lift huge weights, or pick up scents in the air.

Huge cheek teeth grind up food. There are 24, but only four (two seen here on the top jaw) work at a time. Worn-out teeth move forwards and then drop out.

Enormous ears are used for signalling mood and controlling body temperature.

Tusks are giant incisor teeth that grow through an elephant's upper jaw. They are made mainly of ivory.

Leading by example

Elephant herds are based around females and their young. Each herd is led by a senior female, or matriarch, who leads the herd to food or water, following paths that she has memorized over many years. Female calves stay in the herd, but males leave it in their early teens. From then, they live in small groups, meeting females only when they mate. Female African elephants are ready to breed by the age of about ten. They have a single calf, and feed it on milk for three or four years.

Elephants underground
In the mountains of Uganda, forest elephants march deep into caves to feed on salt. In their natural habitat, salty food is hard to find. Instead, they get this essential part of their diet by 'mining' it underground.

Working elephants
African elephants are hard to tame, but Asian elephants have been kept in captivity for thousands of years. They are still used for ceremonial purposes, but now they are becoming rare in the wild.

This elephant is carrying people dressed as historical figures in the Loy Krathong parade, in Thailand.

www.bbc.co.uk/nature/life/african_elephant

"True philosophers are like elephants who, when walking, never place their second foot on the ground until the first is ready."

Bernard le Bovier de Fontenelle (1657–1757)
French writer, from his book Conversations on the Plurality of Worlds *(1686)*

The trunk can suck up water or dust without it getting into the elephant's lungs.

TYPES OF ELEPHANT

The savanna elephant and forest elephant both live in Africa. They have gigantic ears and trunks with two flexible tips. The Asian elephant is smaller, and has a single tip on its trunk.

Asian   **forest**   **savanna**

SWIMMERS AND DIVERS

Most mammals can swim, even though they normally live on dry land. But some kinds are truly at home in water, and get all their food from the sea. Off the coast of California, USA, sea lions and sea otters dive for food among forests of giant kelp, while elephant seals plunge far into the sea's depths to catch fish and squid. Seals and sea lions come ashore to breed, but the sea otter hardly ever sets foot on dry land.

Clash of the giants

Named after their inflatable trunks, male elephant seals can weigh up to three tonnes. During the breeding season they fight for supremacy, rearing up and stabbing with their teeth. After walruses, elephant seals are the largest seals, or pinnipeds.

The fur is silky when young, and short and sleek in adults.

Giant kelp is the world's biggest and fastest-growing seaweed. It forms large, offshore kelp forests.

A sea lion's front teeth include four long, pointed canines and two pointed incisors. Together, these six front teeth give a non-slip grip on the sea lion's prey.

sea lion hunting Pacific whiting – a favourite prey

Hunters in the kelp

Lean, agile and intelligent, the California sea lion is a star performer in the wild and in captivity. It has long front teeth for gripping slippery fish. To swim, it uses its front flippers to propel forwards and its hind ones to steer. On land, it bounds along on all four flippers, with its body off the ground. True seals, or phocids, are more clumsy on the shore. They shuffle along on their stomachs, with their flippers by their sides.

> **PINNIPED** – *a carnivorous mammal with flippers and a streamlined body*

The front flippers have the same bones as a human arm and hand, although in different sizes. A web of leathery skin forms the flipper's blade.

Grazers in the sea

Most diving mammals are carnivorous, but dugongs and manatees eat underwater plants. They live in warm, shallow water and look like giant barrels drifting over the seabed. This dugong (above) is feeding on sea grass off the coast of Western Australia.

LIFE AFLOAT

When sea otters are not diving, they spend a lot of time floating on their backs. It is a strange position for any mammal, but it has a lot of benefits. It lets females keep their young warm and dry. It also turns the otter's stomach into a floating worktop, where it cracks open shells by hitting them against a heavy stone.

sea otter nursing young

sea otter hunting crabs

Offshore otter

The sea otter is the only otter species that lives almost entirely offshore. Diving down into the kelp, it uses its paws to collect small sea animals, deftly avoiding their pincers and spines. Instead of eating on the spot, it carries food to the surface, often tucking it into a fold of skin.

Sea otters stay warm by having the world's densest fur. The hairs trap a layer of air, keeping the skin dry and stopping heat getting out.

www.arkive.org/sea-otter/enhydra-lutris/video-ne08b.html

❯ Elephant seals can dive up to 1.5km deep, and can stay underwater for more than an hour.

The sperm whale's large fluke drives it forwards.

Measuring up to 27m long, the blue whale is by far the world's biggest animal.

Family group

Whales, dolphins and porpoises belong to a single family of mammals, called the cetaceans. There are about 80 different kinds, from the mighty blue whale to the tiny vaquita, which is smaller than most seals. Cetaceans have nostrils, or blowholes, on top of their heads, which close up when they dive. Most cetaceans feed near the surface, but sperm whales and beaked whales dive to great depths to hunt.

WHALES AND DOLPHINS

Roaming the oceans, whales and dolphins spend their whole lives at sea. They include some of the greatest long-distance swimmers, as well as the largest animals. Not all are giants, but they share the same body plan, with streamlined bodies, two front flippers and horizontal flukes, or tails. Most have teeth, but the largest whales are toothless. They filter small animals from water, using mouths that work like giant sieves.

The sperm whale's huge head is filled with waxy oil, which adjusts its buoyancy during dives to feed on giant squid at up to 3,000m deep.

A sperm whale's narrow lower jaw has up to 28 pairs of sharply pointed teeth. Each tooth is up to 20cm long – bigger than any other predator's.

> There are nearly 20 kinds of beaked whales, but many of them have never been seen alive.

The blue whale's brush-like baleen plates trap small animals. The whale then swallows the food using its two-tonne tongue.

River dolphins

With slender jaws and tiny eyes, the boto, or Amazon river dolphin, looks different to sea dolphins. It uses echolocation to find its fish and turtle prey in muddy water. The only other continent where river dolphins are found is Asia.

Male narwhals have long, spiralled tusks, up to 3m long. Males use them like horns in fights with rivals.

Orcas, or killer whales, are large dolphins with a tall fin on their backs. They live in groups, eating seals, sharks and sometimes other whales.

Found worldwide, except near the poles, the bottlenose dolphin is fast, acrobatic and clever. It lives in small groups, or pods, and eats fish and squid.

At just 1.5m, the vaquita is the smallest cetacean. This tiny porpoise lives only in a small area off Mexico and is critically endangered.

⊖ ECHOLOCATION

Toothed cetaceans, such as dolphins and sperm whales, can use sound to find food. They make clicks that travel through the water, and listen for echoes that bounce back from animals. This system, called echolocation, is also used by bats and a small number of other mammals, including shrews.

dolphin sound clicks hitting fish prey

Stranded

Each year, hundreds of whales, such as this pilot whale, are marooned on beaches, where they often die. Strandings happen because whales cannot sense the gradual slope where the seabed rises towards the shore.

http://wwf.panda.org/what_we_do/endangered_species/cetaceans/about/blue_whale

BLUBBER – *a layer of body fat, up to 30cm thick, that sea mammals use to keep themselves warm*

Elastic grooves allow the throat to expand when the whale feeds. The whale filters out fish and krill using its baleen plates. It then tightens the grooves, so that its throat returns to its normal size.

> "Strong against the tide, the enormous whale emerges as he goes."
>
> **Christopher Smart (1722–77)**
> *English poet, from his poem* A Song to David *(1763)*

As the whale bursts upwards, the front flippers make its body spin, while the final push comes from the horizontal fluke, or tail.

The whale's back arches as it rises into the air. Its body rotates and topples back towards the surface.

Whale tracking

Every humpback has unique tail markings. The whales often expose their flukes, so scientists use these markings to identify individual whales. This helps to track humpbacks when they migrate.

OCEAN GIANTS

Weighing up to 40 tonnes, the humpback whale is one of the most extraordinary mammals in the seas. Everything about it is big – from its colossal appetite to its enormous flippers. Humpbacks are famous for their long migrations, and for their amazingly complex underwater songs. They are natural acrobats, bursting upwards through the surface in a manoeuvre called a breach, which ends in one of the biggest splashes in the animal world.

 > Humpback songs can be more than 20 minutes long. They have musical 'trends', which change slowly from year to year.

http://cetus.ucsd.edu/voicesinthesea_org/

Breaching

Many whales breach, but few are as energetic as the humpback. During a breach, the humpback's body may almost entirely leave the water, before twisting and falling, so that it hits the surface on its side. Sometimes a whale breaches just once, but often it performs several breaches in a row for perhaps more than an hour. Scientists are not sure why whales breach. They may use it to attract partners, or perhaps to clean parasites from their skin.

Each eye is about the size of a large orange, and is protected from flowing seawater by a film of transparent oil.

The humpback's two nostrils, or blowholes, close when it dives. They produce a V-shaped plume of water droplets when the whale surfaces and breathes out.

The whale usually makes a half or quarter turn before it hits the surface, while breathing out in a powerful 'blow'.

Picked up an by underwater microphone, this humpback song may have travelled more than 200km through the sea. Humpbacks probably use their songs in courtship, and as a way of keeping in touch.

⊖ BACK FROM THE BRINK

Until the 1960s, the humpback was widely hunted for its meat and its fat, or blubber. More than 90 per cent of the world's humpbacks were killed. Today, humpbacks are protected by most nations and their numbers are recovering slowly. Even so, these whales risk colliding with large ships or getting caught up in fishing gear.

Whale watching has become a major attraction.

KEEPING IN TOUCH

All mammals have to communicate, even if they spend most of their lives on their own. But for meerkats, keeping in touch is a key part of daily life. Meerkats live in groups, or packs, and they use special calls to warn of danger as they search for food. Like most mammals, meerkats also leave signals in scent. These help to mark territory around their burrows, warning other meerkats to stay away.

Martial eagles often weig five times as much as meerkats, and can carry them off in their claws.

An alarm signal for an eagle is a drawn-out call. When sounded, the entire meerkat pack vanishes underground.

The inner lining of the snout is full of nerves sensitive to smells and scent signals, or pheromones.

PHEROMONE – an odour, often working in tiny amounts, that animals use to communicate

> Meerkats have emergency bolt-holes scattered across their territory, just in case they are attacked.

⊖ TREETOP CHORUS

At dawn and dusk, howler monkeys call across the treetops, producing some of the loudest sounds made by any animal on land. These leaf-eating monkeys live in small, slow-moving groups, and they use sound to keep in touch with neighbours. Males have a throat pouch that works like an amplifier, helping calls to carry up to 5km.

female (left) and male (right) howler monkeys calling

Marker mounds

White rhinos leave their dung in communal mounds, called middens, giving the dung a kick to scatter it over the ground. By visiting a midden, a rhino can keep track of other rhinos in the area. It also leaves a signal to show when the rhino last passed by.

Intruder alert

Sentries watch out for danger, and they also sniff the air for meerkats from other groups, which have a 'foreign' smell. Young male meerkats often move to new packs, searching for a chance to breed. Sometimes sentries let them in, but often the pack fights them off.

Adult cobras are dangerous enemies, particularly if they get into the pack's burrows.

"As soon as there is life
there is danger."

Ralph Waldo Emerson (1803–82)
American writer and poet

On the alert

Meerkats live in dry parts of southwest Africa, where they feed on insects and other small animals. They set off in a group, keeping in touch with soft, twittering noises as they fan out over the ground. While most of the pack is busy feeding, sentries stand up on their back legs. They watch and listen, sounding the alarm if any predators or intruders head their way.

Scent signals

Rubbing a low branch with its face, this leopard is leaving a scent mark that will last for many days. The scent contains chemicals called pheromones, which work like a signalling system, allowing it to stay in touch with its own kind.

Propped up by their tails, sentries can keep watch for danger for up to an hour.

APES AND MONKEYS

With grasping hands and forward-facing eyes, apes and monkeys are great climbers, and many spend their lives in trees. Together with lemurs, bushbabies and tarsiers, they belong to a group of mammals called primates, which live mainly in warm parts of the world. Primates often have large brains for their size, and some are experts at solving problems and using tools. We are primates ourselves, and intelligence is one of the secrets of our success.

> PREHENSILE – describes a body part that is able to wrap tightly around something and hang on

The guereza is a leaf-eating monkey from Central and East Africa. It is white when it is born, but gradually changes colour to black and white.

Agile and intelligent, vervet monkeys are a common sight in East and southern Africa. They often come down to the ground, and steal food in towns and on farmland.

Woolly spider monkeys, or muriquis, can feed hanging on by their tails. They live in Brazil's Atlantic forest – a threatened habitat that has almost disappeared.

Like all lemurs, the indri is found only in Madagascar. It leaps from tree to tree with its body upright, and its arms and legs thrown open wide.

Winter warmer

Japanese macaques live further north than any other wild primate. They have extra-long fur to keep out the cold, and in winter they lounge in hot springs to warm up. They are famous for their intelligence, learning new skills and passing them on.

Primates of the world

There are about 250 types of primate. Most live in tropical forests, and although some are vegetarians, many eat a wide range of food, from leaves and fruit to insects and eggs. Primates have long arms and legs, with flexible fingers and toes, and many also have a prehensile tail that can hold all their weight. Eyes that face forwards make primates good at judging distances. This is a vital skill when leaping from branch to branch.

Tarsiers, from Southeast Asia, are tiny primates that hunt insects at night. They watch for prey using their giant eyes, and then leap on it through the dark.

Africa's gorillas are the world's largest primates, weighing up to 200kg. Despite their size and strength, they are harmless vegetarians, spending most of their time on the ground

● MAKING FACES

Over long distances, primates often keep in touch by sound, but when they get together they communicate with their faces as well. This young chimp is making a 'pout' – an expression that means that it is concerned or upset. In chimps, another common expression is the grin. Unlike a human grin, this often means that a chimp is afraid, or keen to prevent a fight.

chimpanzee facial expression

> The smallest primates are mouse lemurs from Madagascar – their bodies can be less than 10cm long.

FOREST LONERS

Orang-utans look different to other apes, with their orange-red fur and amazingly long arms. They feed mainly on fruit and spend almost all of their lives in trees. Unlike chimpanzees and gorillas, they usually live alone, although youngsters stay with their mothers for eight years – one of the longest childhoods in the animal world. They are smart, quick to learn and, despite their size, surprisingly agile.

orang swinging through the trees

Young orangs have light, delicate fur, but adults have coarse fur that is downward-trailing to help to shed the rain. Orang fur colour varies from orange to rusty red.

Holding tight

Orangs are born with a strong grip, and they use it every minute of their lives. Baby orangs cling to their mother's fur, while adults clamber along branches with their leathery hands and feet. As orangs are heavy, they can make slender trees sway under their weight. When a tree bends down, an orang steps off it and grabs one nearby – an efficient way of travelling above the forest floor.

Face flaps

Male orangs can be twice as heavy as females, and develop wide cheek flaps as they mature. They breed from the age of 15, but, unlike females, the males play no part in looking after the young.

"Contrary to general belief, humans imitate apes more than the reverse."

Frans de Waal (born 1948)
Dutch primatologist

> There are two species of orang-utan – one species lives in Sumatra and the other lives in Borneo.

http://animals.nationalgeographic.com/animals/mammals/orangutan

Nesting time

Orangs spend the night in temporary nests, which they build high up in trees. During the day, they roam through the forest, collecting most of their food in the treetops, and only occasionally coming down to the forest floor.

Orang-utans eat more than 100 different types of fruit.

Unlike humans, orangs have opposable big toes. This allows their feet to work like a second set of hands, clinging to branches or supporting their weight.

USING TOOLS

In recent years, scientists have discovered that orangs are at least as good as chimpanzees at making and using tools. They collect insects and honey with specially prepared sticks, and they have even been seen spear-fishing from forested riverbanks. They pass on new skills by watching and copying each other – something that is rare in the animal world.

GOING UNDERGROUND

For small mammals, life in the open can be dangerous, because predators are never far away. To survive, many dig homes underground. Here, they are safe from most of their enemies, although they still have to come to the surface to feed. But some mammals, including moles and mole rats, are fully subterranean. They get everything they need below ground, and hardly ever see the light of day.

Touchy-feely
The star-nosed mole, from North America, finds small animals using a ring of 22 highly sensitive, fleshy tentacles, which spread out around its nose. An expert swimmer, the mole hunts in ponds and streams as well as under the ground.

Loose-fitting skin helps mole rats to squeeze past each other. They huddle together for warmth since they have little body fat.

Mole rats eat large roots, or tubers. They often harvest food a little at a time, so that the plant keeps growing.

new tunnel leading to tuber

final member of the team kicks soil up onto the surface

Team spirit
Beneath the dry grasslands of East Africa, naked mole rats live in permanent groups, or colonies, containing workers ruled by a queen. These odd, bald rodents feed on the swollen roots of plants, using their incisor teeth to tunnel through the soil. A typical family contains up to 80 animals, but only the queen produces young. The workers look after the queen and her offspring, and dig burrows in head-to-tail teams.

active toilet area, or latrine

old latrine, sealed off from burrow system

The queen gives birth to up to 20 pups each time she breeds. She feeds them on milk until the workers take over, giving them solid food.

active latrine

> European badgers inherit their burrows, or setts – some stay in use for more than 100 years.

www.arkive.org/aardvark/orycteropus-afer/video-03b.html

Eyes and ears are small, but the face has highly sensitive whiskers. A mole rat also feels using hairs on its tail.

cluster of untouched tubers

Incisor teeth grow non-stop, making up for wear and tear. Cheeks seal off the mouth behind the incisors, so the mole rat does not swallow the soil.

lead member of the team bites off earth and kicks it backwards

Attack from below

Bursting up through loose sand, a golden mole munches on a locust in Africa's Namib desert. Some golden moles make permanent burrows, but those in deserts 'swim' through sand. They find their prey by listening for faint sounds overhead.

⊖ GIANT BURROWS

With powerful front claws, aardvarks dig record-breaking burrows, wide enough for a person to crawl inside. These pig-like animals from Africa spend the day underground, emerging after dark to feed on termites and ants. Abandoned burrows are often used by other mammals, including warthogs, porcupines and hyenas, and they are favourite areas for snakes.

aardvark emerging from burrow

BEAR FACTS

OMNIVORE - an animal that eats all kinds of food, including meat and plants

With their massive bodies and powerful jaws, bears include the biggest predators on ice and on dry land. The polar bear weighs nearly three-quarters of a tonne. The brown bear is just as large, with enough strength to kill and drag away a horse. Despite their size and strength, most bears are omnivorous, eating all kinds of food. Their menu ranges from fruit and seeds to fish, and even moths.

Bears have average eyesight, but their sense of smell is among the best of all mammals.

Brown bears have impressive incisors but, unlike most carnivores, their rear teeth are shaped for crushing plant food, instead of slicing up meat.

Winter birth

Many bears give birth in winter, which they spend tucked away inside dens. At first, the young are tiny, but they grow fast on their mother's milk. This female black bear has produced three cubs, which will leave her when they are 18 months old.

⊖ LEAFY LUNCH

The giant panda is the only bear that feeds almost entirely on plants. Every day, it eats up to a tenth of its weight in bamboo, sitting upright while it gathers and chews its food. Unlike other bears, each of its front paws has an extra, peg-like 'thumb' that it uses to hold bamboo stems.

panda eating bamboo

> There are eight kinds of bear – the smallest is the sun bear, from Southeast Asia.

www.seemorehd.com/brownbearcam/HDclips

Bear attack

Polar bears are some of the world's most dangerous mammals. They have an exceptionally good sense of smell, and are quickly attracted by the scent of food. This one is trying to bite through a truck window, to get at the driver inside.

Fatal jump

For North America's brown bears, the annual salmon run is an unmissable feast, as millions of fish swim upriver to lay their eggs. Brown bears wade into the fast-flowing rapids, and try to catch the salmon as they leap through the air. Fish is a highly nutritious food, which is why salmon-eating brown bears are bigger than ones that live further inland.

Paws are broad and flat, with strong claws for digging and climbing. Pads of skin give the paws a good grip, even on ice or slippery rocks.

IN THE NIGHT SKY

When darkness falls, some of the strangest animals take to the air. Gliding mammals launch themselves from trees, while bats speed through the dark, homing in on insect prey. Most gliders travel short distances, buoyed by flaps of elastic skin. Bats have real wings, made of leathery skin. They can stay airborne for hours, and some travel hundreds of kilometres when they migrate.

To launch, the glider kicks itself off a tree.

flight membrane has thick edge

large eyes work well in dim light

To steer, the flat underside of the tail acts as a rudder.

To land, the glider's body is steeply angled.

Gliding membrane, or patagium, connects the front and back legs. When not in use, it tightens up along the glider's sides.

Controlled descent

With skin flaps spread wide, the Australian sugar glider moves quickly and silently among the trees. It can travel more than 50m in a single jump, controlling its glide by angling its body and steering with its tail. The sugar glider is a marsupial, but this way of moving is also used by some other mammals, including some rodents and colugos, or flying lemurs.

> Colugos, or flying lemurs, can glide up to 150m – further than any other mammal.

Highly folded nose-leaf emits pulses of ultrasound. Large ears detect echoes that bounce off obstacles and flying insects.

short arm bones close to body

flight membrane connecting tail and legs

The wing membrane is stretched by thin and unusually flexible finger bones, which flick as the wing beats. This helps the bat to zigzag through the air.

thin layer of double-sided skin

Powered flight

Bats are the only mammals with wings, and the only ones that use their own muscle power to stay in the air. Predatory kinds, or microbats, are extremely agile fliers. They find their prey by echolocation – the same system used by dolphins and whales – and often use their wings and tail to scoop prey towards their mouths.

flying insect prey found through echolocation

www.nhm.ac.uk/nature-online/life/mammals/bats

Fishing in the dark

Swooping low over the water, a Mexican bulldog bat snatches up a fish. Fish-eating bats sense ripples on the surface of lakes and ponds, and use them to home in on their prey.

⊖ PRIVATE SHELTERS

During the day, most insect-eating bats hide away in tree-holes or in caves. These white tent-making bats, from Central America, have another way of staying out of sight. They bite through the underside of a large leaf, so that its sides drop down. The bats then crowd together inside, staying warm and dry.

tent-making bats under a leaf

Ready for take-off

Flying foxes look quite different to bats that hunt insects. As well as being big, they have dog-like faces and big eyes, sturdy back legs and a long, bony thumb on each wing. When they are resting, they often wrap their wings around their bodies like a coat. Females keep their young warm and safe by tucking them up inside.

Wings normally overlap when resting. If the bats gets too warm, it opens them wide, and licks them to cool down.

FLYING GIANTS

With wings up to 1.8m across, flying foxes are bigger than most birds. Despite the name, they are not foxes, but megabats – giant vegetarians that feed on fruits and flowers. Taking off as the sun sets, they speed over the treetops, using sight and smell to find food. Unlike most bats, flying foxes spend the day hanging from exposed branches high up in trees. These roosts, called camps, are full of activity, particularly during the breeding season.

A mother bat wraps up her young in her wings.

> In Africa, some megabats migrate in 'flocks' numbering hundreds of thousands of animals.

The wing membrane is light but tough, so that it does not tear when the bat lands in trees.

Flying foxes have a claw on their thumbs, and on the second finger of each wing. They use their two thumb claws to walk upside down along branches, and to get at food.

www.arkive.org/black-flying-fox/pteropus-alecto/video-02.html

A flexible neck lets the bat look all around while hanging upside down.

Messy eaters

Flying foxes are noisy and untidy feeders. They crash-land in trees and feed by lapping up pollen and nectar, or by chewing fruit into a pulp. After swallowing the juice, they spit out the seeds, helping trees to spread.

⊖ DANGER ZONE

Despite their size, flying foxes have a lot of enemies. During the daytime, they are attacked by eagles and other birds of prey. After dark, they are ambushed by snakes and owls. With their giant wings, they also get tangled up in power lines, and in nets that farmers use to protect their fruit crops.

carpet python at a flying fox camp

helicopter arriving to move the white rhino

MAMMALS IN DANGER

Whale wars

Since 1986, whales have been protected by a hunting ban, which forbids commercial whaling. Despite this, some hunting continues. In 2007, these inflatable whales in Sydney, Australia, were a protest against a decision by Japan to resume killing humpback whales.

Today, wild mammals face difficult problems. Many are threatened by disappearing forests, hunting, pollution and climate change. The danger list includes some of the world's best-known creatures – such as tigers, rhinos and giant pandas – as well as lots of smaller mammals that rarely make the headlines. Fortunately, the news is not all bad. Around the world, conservation projects are helping some critically threatened mammals to survive.

CAPTIVE BREEDING – when species breed in captivity and are later released into the wild

The three-tonne rhino is heavily sedated, then rolled onto a net, which will be slung beneath the helicopter.

> The Javan rhino is one of the world's rarest mammals – only about 50 are left in the wild.

Airlift

With nearly 18,000 animals in game parks and sanctuaries, the white rhino is off the danger list, but its survival depends on round-the-clock conservation. The main threat comes from poachers, who target white rhinos for their horns, one of which can be sold for thousands of dollars. As well as being protected, rhinos are actively managed to help their numbers grow. In South Africa, 'spare' adults are flown by helicopter to new areas to expand the rhino's range.

Ear notching is a quick and relatively painless way of identifying a rhino. The notches are permanent, and easy to see with binoculars.

Primate crisis

In the next 50 years, more than half the world's primates, including orang-utans, could die out in the wild. For most, the biggest threat is the destruction of their forest habitat, as people cut down trees for timber and to clear land for farming.

white rhino and calf

Back from the edge

Over the centuries, many horses escaped into the wild, but only Przewalski's horses from Mongolia are truly wild animals. They were saved from extinction in the 20th century through captive breeding. About 300 now live in the wild.

⊖ CAUGHT ON CAMERA

On the Asian island of Borneo, a rare Sundaland clouded leopard triggers off an automatic camera on the forest floor. This kind of equipment is making it easier to keep track of endangered species, and to discover ones that are entirely new to science. This is particularly true in forests and the deep ocean, where it is easy for animals to stay hidden.

Sundaland clouded leopard

GLOSSARY

altitude
Height above sea level. Most mammals live below 5,000m – above this, few survive the cold or the thin air.

barb
A backward-pointing scale that makes something more difficult to dislodge.

breed
To have offspring. Before mammals can breed, parents have to pair up and mate.

buoyancy
A force that stops things sinking. Most mammals are naturally buoyant, but some swimming mammals can reduce their buoyancy when they dive.

burrow
A home that is dug out underground. Many mammals dig their own burrows, using their feet or their teeth, but some take over burrows that have been abandoned by other animals.

canine
A pointed front tooth that mammalian carnivores use to grip their prey.

carnassial
A blade-like tooth that mammalian carnivores use to slice up meat.

carnivore
Any animal that eats meat. In mammals, the same word is also used for the family that includes cats, dogs, wolves and their relatives.

cell
Cells are the microscopic units that make up all living things. A mammal's body contains more than 200 types of cell – each one has a different range of tasks.

colony
A group of animals, from the same species, that live together in an extended family.

courtship
Special forms of behaviour animals use during the breeding season, to help them to attract a partner.

dominant
A high-ranking animal within a group. In lions, wolves and many other mammals, only the dominant animals breed.

echolocation
Sensing food, or the way ahead, by making short bursts of sound and listening for echoes that come back.

fluke
The tail of a whale or a dolphin. Unlike a fish's tail, flukes are horizontal, and they do not contain any hard struts or bones.

glands
A small organ, in an animal's body or on its skin, which makes and releases special chemicals.

gnaw
To chew through food or obstacles using self-sharpening incisors, or front teeth.

herd
A group of mammals that stays together for most of their lives. Herds are usually made up of plant-eating mammals with hooves.

hibernation
A special kind of deep, winter sleep. It lets animals survive cold weather, using food stored inside their bodies.

hoof
A toe with a hard tip, made of the same substance found in fingernails. Hooves are found in large, plant-eating mammals, and they keep growing to make up for wear and tear.

ce age

A long period of intense cold, causing glaciers and ice caps to expand. The last ice age ended about 10,000 years ago.

ncisor

ncisors are flat-edged front teeth that mammals use to nip and to gnaw.

nstinct

Behaviour that is built into a mammal's nervous system, and so is not learned.

krill

Finger-sized relatives of shrimps that ive in huge swarms in polar seas. They make up an important source of food for whales and seals.

mammoth

A prehistoric member of the elephant family. Ice-age mammoths were often covered with long fur.

marsupial

A mammal that raises its young in a pouch. Most marsupials live in Australia and New Guinea, but some are found in the Americas.

membrane

A thin layer of living tissue, usually with its own blood supply and nerves.

migration

A long return journey between two parts of the world. Animals usually migrate with the seasons, so that they arrive at a good time to feed and breed.

nutritious

Full of nutrients – the substances that fuel an animal's body and let it grow.

omnivore

An animal that eats all kinds of food.

parasite

An animal that spends its life on or inside a much bigger animal, using it for food. Many parasites that attack mammals feed on their blood.

predator

An animal that hunts for its food.

prey

An animal that predators hunt for food.

rodent

A small or medium-sized mammal with front teeth that are specially shaped for gnawing.

species

A group of living things that look alike, and that breed only with their own kind.

stamina

Endurance or staying power. Many predatory mammals use stamina to out-run their prey.

streamlined

Having a smooth outline that slips easily through water or through air. Streamlining is particularly important for predators, such as sea lions, because they have to move fast to catch their prey.

subterranean

Anything that is underground.

territory

A piece of ground that an animal claims as its own, keeping rivals away. It usually contains enough food and space to raise a family.

tundra

The cold, treeless landscape found around the Arctic, and near to the tops of many mountains.

ultrasound

Pulses of sound that are too high-pitched for human ears to hear. Bats, dolphins and other mammals use ultrasound to locate their food.

INDEX

A
aardvarks 35
Africa 4, 6, 12, 16, 20, 21, 29, 30, 31, 34, 35, 40, 43
alpha animals 10
ancient mammals 4, 13, 20
anteaters 4, 8
antelopes 16
apes 30–31, 32
  chimpanzees 31, 32, 33
  gorillas 31, 32
  orang-utans 32–33, 43
Arctic 17, 18, 19
armadillos 13
armoured mammals 12, 13
Asia 4, 5, 18, 19, 21, 25, 30, 31, 32, 36, 40, 42, 43
Australia 23, 38, 40, 42

B
badgers 34
baleen 24, 25, 27
barbs 12, 44
bats 4, 19, 38, 39, 40–41
bears 8, 36–37
  black bears 36
  brown bears 36, 37
  grizzly bears 8
  pandas 36, 42
  polar bears 36, 37
  sun bears 36

birth 6–7, 16, 17, 36
blowholes 24, 27
bones 8, 9, 14, 20, 22, 23, 39
breeding 6–7, 10, 14, 16, 21, 22, 32, 40, 42, 43, 44
burrows 14, 18, 19, 28, 29, 34, 35, 44
bushbabies 30

C
camels 18–19
captivity 21, 22
caribou 16, 17
carnivores 5, 8, 9, 22, 23, 25, 36, 44
cats 8, 13
  leopards 29, 43
  lions 12, 13
  pumas 8–9
  tigers 5, 42
caves 19, 21, 39
cells 18, 44
Central America 25, 39
cetaceans 24, 25
  see also dolphins, whales
claws 7, 13, 28, 35, 37, 41
colonies 34, 44
colugos 38
communication 11, 27, 28–29, 31
conservation 42–43

D
deer 10, 17
deserts 18, 19, 35
dogs 10
dolphins 8, 24–25
dugongs 23

E
ears 8, 10, 20, 21
echidnas 6
echolocation 25, 39, 44
egg-laying mammals 6
elephants 4, 20–21
endangered animals 25, 43
eyes 10, 15, 25, 27, 31, 35, 38

F
farm animals 16
fat 4, 18, 19, 27, 34
fighting 16, 22, 25
filter-feeding 24, 25, 27
flippers 22, 23, 24, 26
flying 38, 39
food 6, 8, 15, 16, 18
  fish 8, 22, 25, 26, 27, 33, 37, 39
  fruit 4, 31, 32, 40, 41
  insects 8, 18, 29, 31, 33, 35, 38, 39
  meat 5, 9, 11

plants 14, 23, 31, 34, 36
  seeds 14, 18
forests 17, 33, 43
foxes, Arctic 19
fur 4, 7, 14, 18, 19, 22, 23, 30, 32

G
gazelles 17
giraffes 4
glands 13, 14, 16, 44
gliders 38
grasslands 6, 16

H
hair 4, 12, 19, 23, 35
herds 16, 17, 21, 44
hibernation 18, 19, 44
hooves 5, 16, 44
horns 16, 17, 43
horses, Przewalski's 43
humans, as mammals 5, 18, 30, 32
hyenas 8, 35

IJ
instincts 7, 16, 45

KL
kangaroos 5, 7
krill 26, 45
lemurs 5, 30, 31

INVESTIGATE

Find out about living mammals by visiting zoos and wildlife parks.
Museums are also a great way to discover mammals from the past.

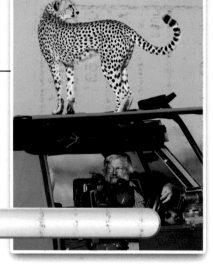

A young chimp
plays on a zoo
climbing frame.

Wildlife parks and zoos

Modern zoos give mammals lots of space, and a habitat like their natural home.
In wildlife parks, animals have more room to roam, letting them behave as if wild.

**Ice-age mammoths had
extra-long fur, protecting
them against the bitter cold.**

📖 *What's it like to be a...? Zoo Keeper* by Elizabeth Dowen
(A & C Black)

✦ Whipsnade Zoo, Dunstable, Bedfordshire, LU6 2LF, UK

🌐 www.zsl.org/zsl-whipsnade-zoo

Museums and exhibitions

Most big natural history museums have displays showing
how wild mammals live. Some also have fossils of prehistoric
species, including giant kinds that lived during the last ice age.

📖 *National Geographic Prehistoric Mammals* by Alan Turner
(National Geographic)

✦ Natural History Museum, Cromwell Road, London,
SW7 5BD, UK

🌐 www.nhm.ac.uk/visit-us/galleries/blue-zone/mammals

**A cheetah watches
for prey from a truck,
during filming for
a documentary.**

Documentaries and films

**Despite protection, tigers are
still endangered, and face an
uncertain future in the wild.**

See some of the world's most spectacular mammals in close-up,
thanks to documentaries and films. If you've got a camera, try
taking your own photos of wild mammals in your area.

📖 *Nature Photography* by Christopher Weston (Focal Press)

✦ *The Life of Mammals* DVD (2 Entertain Video)

🌐 www.meerkatmanor.co.uk/index.htm

Conservation groups

Many conservation organizations help to protect mammals. Some are focused on
individual species, while others aim to conserve all mammals in a country or region.

📖 *Lions, Tigers and Bears: Why are Big Predators so Rare?* by Ron Hirshi (Boyds Mills Press)

✦ The Mammal Society, 3 The Carronades, New Road, Southampton, SO14 0AA, UK

🌐 www.panthera.org/programs/tiger/save-tiger-fund